There Once Was a Bug...

A Children's Approach to the Characteristics of the Insect Phylogeny

A note to parents and readers:

This book is full of fun information on insects! There are some big words, but don't worry! There is a glossary in the back of the book where you can learn all about those big words and how to pronounce them. Parents, join the fun with your children and learn together!

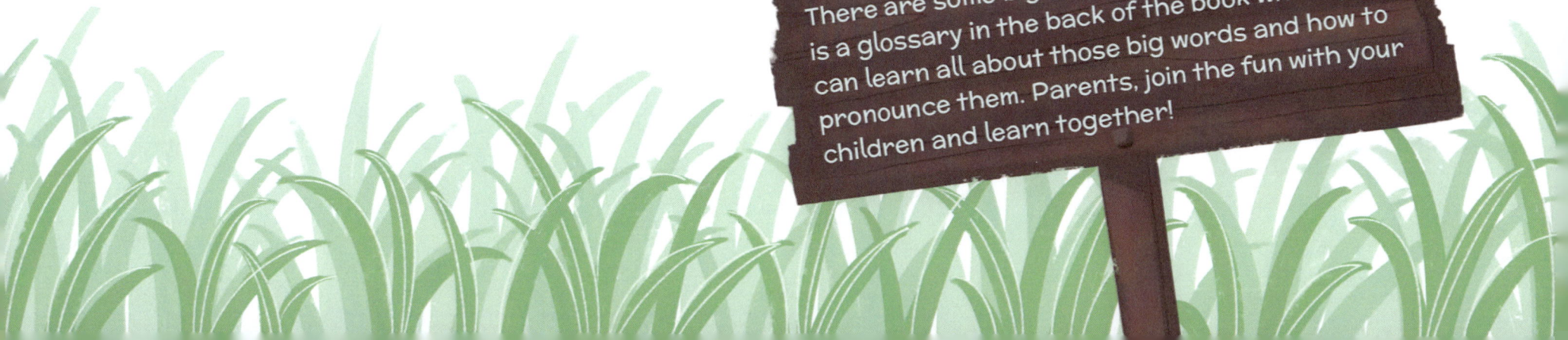

Collembola
(kuh–LEM–buh–luh)

There once was a

collembolan

who liked to

spring,

sprang,

and sprung!

Her furcula and retinaculum

helped her have all that fun!

Springtails

Protura
(pro–TUR–uh)

There once was a
proturan

who liked to put
his legs ahead.

His legs up there

helped him sense
where he'd tread!

Coneheads

Diplura
(di-PLUR-uh)

There once was a dipluran

who had two cerci at her end.

It's how she got her name,

which is easy to comprehend!

Two-pronged Bristletails

Archaeognatha
(ar–kee–og–NAY–thuh)

There once was an archaeognathan

who liked to leap, bound, and jump!

That's so much easier

with his thorax shaped like a hump!

Jumping Bristletails

Zygentoma

(zy-gen-TOE-muh)

There once was a zygentoman

who had a body oh-so flat.

Living in your bathroom

is where you'll find her at!

Silverfish, Firebrats

Odonata
(o–duh–NAH–tuh)

There once was an
odonate

who used his legs while
he would fly

to grab his sneaky prey

from right out of the
sky!

Dragonflies, Damselflies

Ephemeroptera
(uh–FEM–er–OP–ter–uh)

There once was an ephemeropteran

who liked to swarm, grasp, and play!

Unfortunately, this would last

only for a day!

Mayflies

Zoraptera

(zor-APP-ter-uh)

There once was a zorapteran

who liked to live around wood.

That's all I can tell you

because they're not well understood!

Angel Insects

Dermaptera

(der–MAP–ter–uh)

There once was a
dermapteran

who was only active
at night

and had two pincers

to help him fight!

Earwigs

Orthoptera
(or–THOP–ter–uh)

There once was an orthopteran

who liked to sing his favorite song.

To call out to his friends,

he would sing all night long!

Grasshoppers, Locusts, Katydids, Crickets

Plecoptera
(pleh–COP–ter–uh)

There once was a plecopteran

who liked to spend time by the stream.

When she brought her friends along,

it meant the water was clean!

Stoneflies

Mantophasmatodea

(man-toe-FAZ-muh-TOE-dee-uh)

There once was a mantophasmatodean

who was wingless and called "Heel-walker."

Since he is predacious,

you could also call him "Insect-stalker!"

Heel-walkers

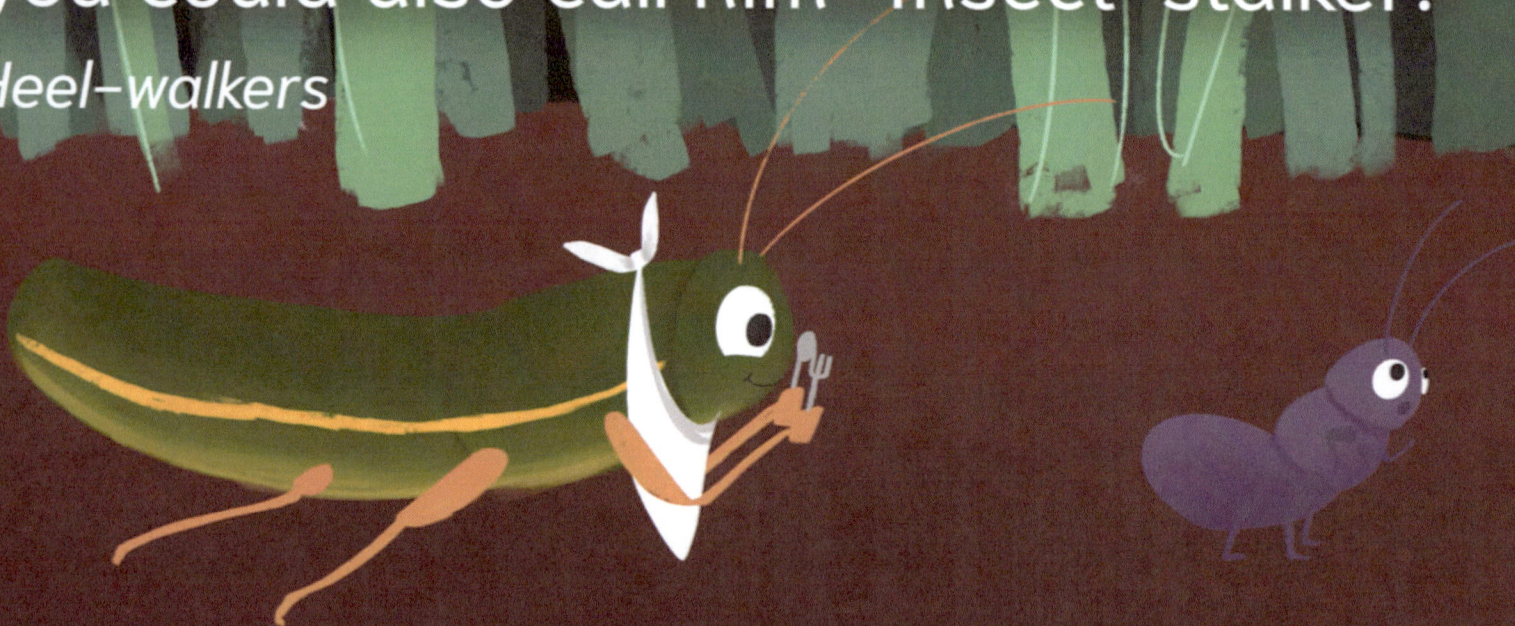

Grylloblattodea
(GRIL–LO–blat–TOE–dee–uh)

There once was a grylloblattid

who liked to live in cold and ice.

Her species is threatened,

so if you see her, be nice!

Ice Crawlers

Embioptera

(em-bee-OP-ter-uh)

There once was an embiopteran who liked to spin silk tunnels. No predator could get to her through those maze-like funnels!
Webspinners

Phasmatodea
(faz–muh–TOE–dee–uh)

There once was a phasmid

who liked to look like
different plants.

She could look like a stick
or leaf,

and that's not
happenstance!

Stick Insects, Leaf Insects

Mantodea
(man–TOE–dee–uh)

There once was a mantid

who hunted with legs raptorial.

Some hunting strategies are

generalist, ambush, and cursorial!

Mantises

Blattodea
(bluh–TOE–dee–uh)

There once was a blattodean

who did not like to live alone,

so he brought all his friends

to live with you in your home!
Cockroaches, Termites

Psocodea
(so–COH–dee–uh)

There once was a psocid

who had a bulb on her head

and held her wings roof–like

instead of outspread!

Booklice, Barklice, Parasitic Lice

Thysanoptera
(THIGH–san–OP–ter–uh)

There once was a thysanopteran

who had wings that were kind of feathery,

but using those wings to fly around

was not a guarantee!

Thrips

Hemiptera

(hem–IP–ter–uh)

There once was a
hemipteran

who had mouthparts
used to suck.

If he could get a meal,

then he was in luck!

True Bugs

Hymenoptera

(HIGH–men–OP–ter–uh)

There once was a hymenopteran

with an ovipositor as a stinger.

If she lands on you,

don't let her linger!

Ants, Wasps, Bees

Raphidioptera

(ruh-FID-EE-op-ter-uh)

There once was a
raphidiopteran

whose ovipositor and
neck made her snake-like.

She could capture her
prey quickly

with a fast head-strike!

Snakeflies

Neuroptera
(NUR–op–ter–uh)

There once was a neuropteran

who had veins in his wings like a net.

The pattern is not one

you would soon forget!
Lacewings, Mantidflies, Antlions, and Friends

Megaloptera
(meg-uh-LOP-ter-uh)

There once was a megalopteran

who as a larva had gills.

Now a grown adult,

he lives by the water still!

Dobsonflies, Alderflies, Fishflies

Strepsiptera
(strep–SIP–ter–uh)

There once was a strepsipteran

who had wings that were all twisted.

What a weird bug

to ever have existed!
Twisted-wing Parasites

Coleoptera
(coh–lee–OP–ter–uh)

There once was a coleopteran

with a set of wings that were hard.

You can find many different kinds

outside in your yard!
Beetles

Mecoptera
(meh–COP–ter–uh)

There once was a mecopteran

who had a rostrum very long.

At its end were chewing mouthparts

to eat his food all gone!

Scorpionflies, Hangingflies

Siphonaptera
(sigh-fun-APP-ter-uh)

There once was a siphonapteran

who liked to live as a parasite.

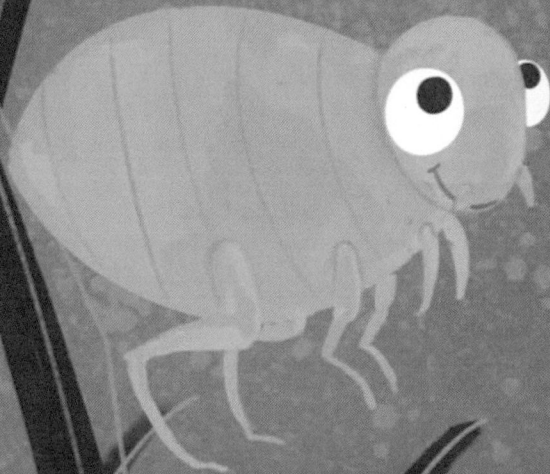

She got her food from birds and mammals

through a simple bite!

Fleas

Diptera
(DIP-ter-uh)

There once was a dipteran

who had behind each wing a haltere

that served to help her

balance,

fly,

and steer!

Flies

Trichoptera
(tri-COP-ter-uh)

There once was a
trichopteran

who made cases out of
pebbles, sticks, and leaves.

He changed from larva to
pupa

while living in those sleeves!

Caddisflies

Lepidoptera

(leh-pid-OP-ter-uh)

There once was a lepidopteran

who was covered in scales

that gave both her wings

beautiful details!

Butterflies, Moths

Glossary

Adult (UH-duhlt). The adult stage of the insect's life cycle is like the grown-up stage of the human life cycle! The adult stage is the last stage in the insect life cycle, which means these bugs are all grown up and can mate! Some insects become adults by going through a big change called complete metamorphosis. For these insects, the adult stage is after the pupal stage. Other insects have an incomplete metamorphosis. These insects become adults after growing up from the nymphal stage.

Ambush (AM-bush). Ambush hunting is one way some insects get their food. The hungry insect waits until the bug it wants to eat comes close. Then, it surprises and grabs the bug! Some insect predators that use the ambush strategy are praying mantids (Order Mantodea) and antlion larvae (Order Neuroptera).

Cerci (SER-sigh). Cerci can look like two little tails or pincers on the end of an insect's body. When the cerci look like pincers, they can help the insect capture prey or defend themselves, like we see in earwigs (Order Dermaptera).

Cursorial (kur-SOR-ee-uhl). Cursorial hunting is one way some insects get their food on the ground. The hungry insect chases after the bug it wants to eat. For example, tiger beetles (Order Coleoptera) use their long legs to run really fast and catch their prey!

Furcula (FUR-cue-luh). The furcula is the forked-looking part of a springtail's body (Order Collembola) that launches the springtail high into the air! The retinaculum holds the furcula in place until it is time for the springtail to spring, sprang, and sprung!

Generalist (JEN-er-uhl-list). Generalist hunting is another way some insects get their food. These hungry insects are not picky eaters and will eat many different bugs and hunt them any way they can! Praying mantids (Order Mantodea) are generalists because they will eat almost any insect they catch.

Gills (gilz). Gills are like tiny, feathery lungs found on larvae that live underwater. The gills take in the oxygen from the water so the larva can breathe!

Haltere (HALL-teer). Halteres are like little knobs found by the wings of some insects. In flies (Order Diptera), the halteres are behind their wings, but in twisted-wing parasites (Order Strepsiptera), the halteres are found in front of their wings. Halteres move really fast when the insect flies to help the bug balance and move where it wants to go!

Insect (IN-sekt). Insects are small animals that don't have any bones in their body! Instead, they have a hard outer covering like a suit of armor that protects them! Insect bodies have three parts. This first part is their head, which has their eyes and antennae. The second part is their thorax, where their six legs and wings attach. The third part is their abdomen, which holds all their organs. Some insects have wings to help them fly, while others just use their legs to crawl around! There are more insects than any other kind of animal in the world!

Larva (LAR-vuh). The larval stage of an insect's life cycle is like the kid stage of the human life cycle! An insect is a larva when it leaves the egg. A larva will look different than its adult form until it grows up and changes into an adult through a process called complete metamorphosis! For example, a caterpillar is in the larval stage of a butterfly (Order Lepidoptera). Some insects have an incomplete metamorphosis instead. When these insects leave the egg, their kid stage is called the nymphal stage, not the larval stage! Unlike larvae, nymphs will look like tiny versions of their adult form as they grow up! For example, grasshopper nymphs look like mini adult grasshoppers (Order Orthoptera).

Mouthparts (mouth-parts). Mouthparts are what insects use to eat their food! Insects have different types of mouthparts based on what they eat. For example, insects with chewing mouthparts eat plants or other bugs, and insects with piercing-sucking mouthparts eat blood, plant sap, or nectar.

Ovipositor (OH-vi-POZ-i-tur). The ovipositor is the long-looking tube at the end of a female insect's body that she uses to lay eggs. In some insects like bees and wasps (Order Hymenoptera), the ovipositor acts as a stinger to help the insect defend itself!

Parasite (PARE-uh-site). A parasite is not a very nice houseguest! It is an insect that gets its food from and makes its home in or on its host. You may be familiar with the parasites called fleas (Order Siphonaptera) if they've ever made their home on your household pet!

Phylogeny (fy-LOJ-uh-nee). A phylogeny is like a giant family tree for all the bugs in the world! Scientists study how insects look and act and put them in the same group if they have similar features. In this book, we learned about some of the characteristics of these groups, called insect orders. For example, grasshoppers, locusts, katydids, and crickets are all grouped together in the insect order Orthoptera because of their similarities. By studying this phylogeny or big bug family tree, we can learn how all the different insects are related to each other and how they all came from the same super old grandparent bug!

Predator (PREH-duh-tur)/**Predacious** (preh-DAY-shuhs). A predacious insect acts as a predator and hunts other insects for food. For example, the heel-walker (Order Mantophasmatodea) is a predator because it hunts for different kinds of insects to eat.

Prey (pray). A prey is an insect that is always running for its life! A prey gets hunted and is food for hungry insect predators. For example, mosquitoes (Order Diptera) are prey for dragonflies (Order Odonata) because dragonflies hunt and eat mosquitoes.

Pupa (PEW–puh). The pupal stage of an insect's life cycle is like the teenage stage of the human life cycle! An insect is a pupa after it grows from a larva and before it goes through complete metamorphosis into the final life stage of an adult. For example, caddisfly (Order Trichoptera) larvae build cases and live in them while becoming pupae. Once leaving the case, the caddisflies can finish growing into their adult form.

Raptorial (rap–TOR–ee–uhl). An insect's legs are raptorial when they are shaped in a way that helps the hungry insect grab its prey and hold it tight! Some insects that have raptorial legs are praying mantids (Order Mantodea), giant water bugs (Order Hemiptera), and mantidflies (Order Neuroptera).

Retinaculum (ret–in–ACK–cue–lum). The retinaculum is the part of a springtail's body (Order Collembola) that holds the furcula in place. When the springtail is ready to spring into the air, the retinaculum releases the furcula, and up it goes!

Rostrum (ROST–rum). A rostrum is the long, snout–looking part of an insect's head where you can find the insect's mouthparts. Some insects with a rostrum are scorpionflies (Order Mecoptera), hangingflies (Order Mecoptera), and weevils (Order Coleoptera).

Thorax (THOR–acks). The thorax is the middle part of an insect's body that comes after the head and before the abdomen. The insect's wings and legs are attached to the thorax.

Threatened (THRET–end). Threatened insects don't have a lot of their own kind and can go extinct more easily. To learn more about some of the threatened insect species in the world, you can visit The International Union for Conservation of Nature's Red List of Threatened Species by visiting iucnredlist.org.

Dedications

To Brayden, a bug–fearer who spent a semester collecting insects with me and who has always encouraged me. To Christopher, a bug–lover who thinks every insect he sees is a "bee."–Kate

To my family, thank you for always being on my team and cheering me on. I wouldn't be where I am without you guys. I love you! –Ashley

Acknowledgements

A very special thank you to Dr. Michael F. Whiting whose teachings inspired this book and who was a great source of information, encouragement, and help.

Disclaimers

The information in this book was correct at the time of publication, but neither the Author nor June Books, LLC assume any liability for loss or damage caused by errors or omissions.

Identifiers
LCCN: 2023924213
Hardcover ISBN: 979-8-9896574-0-7
Paperback ISBN: 979-8-9896574-1-4

www.ingramcontent.com/pod-product-compliance
Lightning Source LLC
Chambersburg PA
CBRC091141030426
42335CB00009B/208